SCHOLASTIC

writing guides

With interactive resources on CD-ROM

Funny Stories

for ages

5-7

Hilary Braund,
Jean Evans and
Deborah Gibbon

Credits

Authors
Hilary Braund, Jean Evans
and Deborah Gibbon

Development Editors
Rachel Mackinnon and
Marion Archer

Assistant Editor
Sarah Sodhi

Series Designer
Anna Oliwa

Designers
Paul Stockmans and
Liz Gilbert

Cover Illustration
Mark Oliver

Illustrations
Mike Phillips and
Arthur Robins

CD-ROM Development
CD-ROM developed in
association with Infuze Ltd

Mixed Sources
Product group from well-managed
forests and other controlled sources
www.fsc.org Cert no. TT-COC-002769
© 1996 Forest Stewardship Council
FSC

Text © 2010 Jean Evans
Text © 2002, 2010 Hilary Braund and Deborah Gibbon
© 2010 Scholastic Ltd

Designed using Adobe InDesign

Published by Scholastic Ltd,
Book End
Range Road
Witney
Oxfordshire
OX29 0YD
www.scholastic.co.uk

Printed by Bell & Bain

1 2 3 4 5 6 7 8 9   0 1 2 3 4 5 6 7 8 9

British Library Cataloguing-in-Publication Data
A catalogue record for this book is available from the British Library.

ISBN 978-1407-11255-8

Acknowledgments
The publishers gratefully acknowledge permission to reproduce the following copyright material: **Simon James** for the use of an extract and illustrations from *The Day Jake Vacuumed* by Simon James © 1989, Simon James (1989, Picture Piper, JM Dent and Sons Ltd). **Walker Books** for the use of an extract from *Little Rabbit Foo Foo* by Michael Rosen © 1990, Michael Rosen (1990, Walker Books). **The Watts Publishing Group** for the use of an extract from *Mr Bear Babysits* by Debi Gliori © 1994, Debi Gliori (1994, Orchard Books).
Every effort has been made to trace copyright holders for the works reproduced in this book, and the publisher apologise for any inadvertent omissions.

CD-ROM Minimum specifications:

Windows 2000/XP/Vista	Mac OSX 10.4	
Processor: 1 GHz	RAM: 512 MB	Graphics card: 32bit
Audio card: Yes	CD-ROM drive speed: 8x	Hard disk space: 200MB
Screen resolution: 800x600		

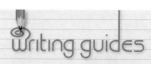

Contents

Introduction: Funny Stories

The *Writing Guides* series aims to inspire and motivate children as writers by using creative approaches. Each *Writing Guide* contains activities and photocopiable resources designed to develop children's understanding of a particular genre (for example, fairy stories). The activities are in line with the requirements of the National Curriculum and the recommendations in the *Primary Framework for Literacy*. The teacher resource books are accompanied by a CD-ROM containing a range of interactive activities and resources.

What's in the book?

The *Writing Guides* series provides a structured approach to developing children's writing. Each book is divided into four sections.

Section 1: **Using good examples**
Three text extracts are provided to explore the typical features of the genre.

Section 2: **Developing writing**
There are ten short, focussed writing tasks in this section. These are designed to develop children's ability to use the key features of the genre in their own writing. The teachers' notes explain the objective of each activity and provide guidance on delivery, including how to use the photocopiable pages and the materials on the CD-ROM.

Section 3: **Writing**
The three writing projects in this section require the children to produce an extended piece of writing using the key features of the genre.

Section 4: **Review**
This section consists of a 'Self review', 'Peer review' and 'Teacher review'. These can be used to evaluate how effectively the children have met the writing criteria for the genre.

What's on the CD-ROM?

The accompanying CD-ROM contains a range of motivating activities and resources. The activities can be used for independent work or can be used on an interactive whiteboard to enhance group teaching.
Each CD-ROM contains:
- three text extracts that illustrate the typical features of the genre
- interactive versions of selected photocopiable pages
- four photographs and an audio file to create imaginative contexts for writing
- a selection of writing templates and images which can be used to produce extended pieces of writing.

The interactive activities on the CD-ROM promote active learning and support a range of teaching approaches and learning styles. For example, drag and drop and sequencing activities will support kinaesthetic learners.

Talk for writing

Each *Writing Guide* uses the principles of 'Talk for writing' to support children's writing development by providing opportunities for them to rehearse ideas orally in preparation for writing. 'Talk for writing' is promoted using a variety of teaching strategies including discussions, questioning and drama activities (such as, developing imaginative dialogue – see *Fantasy Stories for Ages 9–11*).

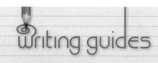

How to use the CD-ROM

Start screen: click on the 'Start' button to go to the main menu.

This section contains brief instructions on how to use the CD-ROM. For more detailed guidance, go to 'How to use the CD-ROM' on the start screen or click on the 'Help' button located in the top right-hand corner of the screen.

Installing the CD-ROM

Follow the instructions on the disk to install the CD-ROM onto your computer. Once the CD-ROM is installed, navigate to the program location and double click on the program icon to open it.

Main menu screen

Main menu

The main menu provides links to all of the writing activities and resources on the CD-ROM. Clicking on a button from the main menu will take you to a sub-menu that lists all of the activities and resources in that section. From here you have the option to 'Launch' the interactive activities, which may contain more than one screen, or print out the activities for pupils to complete by hand.

If you wish to return to a previous menu, click the 'Menu' button in the top right-hand corner of the screen; this acts as a 'back' button.

Screen tools

A range of simple writing tools that can be used in all of the writing activities are contained in the toolbar at the bottom of the screen.

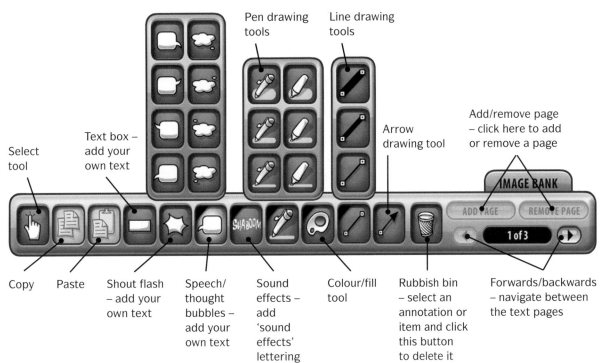

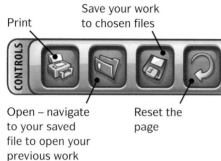

Print

Save your work to chosen files

Open – navigate to your saved file to open your previous work

Reset the page

Printing and saving work

All of the resources on the CD-ROM are printable. You can also save and retrieve any annotations made on the writing activities. Click on the 'Controls' tab on the right-hand side of the screen to access the 'Print', 'Open', 'Save' and 'Reset screen' buttons.

View all thumbnails by clicking on the arrows

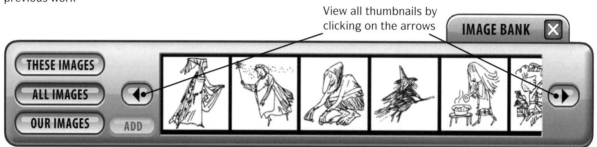

Image bank – click and drag an image to add it to an activity

Image bank

Each CD-ROM has an 'Image bank' containing images appropriate to the genre being taught. Click on the tab at the bottom right of the screen to open the 'Image bank'. On the left-hand side there are three large buttons.

- The 'These images' button will display only the images associated with the specific activity currently open.
- The 'All images' button will display all the photographs and illustrations available on the CD-ROM.
- The 'Our images' button will contain any images you or the children have added to the CD-ROM.

Press the left or right arrows to scroll through the images available. Select an image and drag and drop it into the desired location on the screen. If necessary, resize the image using the arrow icon that appears at the bottom right of the image.

You can upload images to the 'Image bank', including digital photographs or images drawn and scanned into the computer. Click on 'Our images' and then 'Add' to navigate to where the image is stored. A thumbnail picture will be added to the gallery.

Writing your own story

Each CD-ROM contains a selection of blank writing templates. The fiction genre templates will be categorised under the button 'My story' and the non-fiction templates will be categorised under 'My recount' or 'My writing'. The writing templates encourage the children to produce an extended piece of genre writing. They can also add images, speech bubbles and use other tools to enhance their work.

The fiction titles also include a cover template for the children to use. They can customise their cover by adding their own title, blurb and images.

Section 1
Using good examples

Using funny stories

There is a vast range of funny stories written for young children. While the format and presentation may vary, the sources of humour can often be traced to common strands, as identified in the key features box.

The characters chosen by the author are often a key source of humour. Just when we anticipate an ordinary response to a situation, a character might suddenly behave outrageously. This element of surprise underpins many of our funniest stories. Characters can become muddled, get things wrong and generally insert visual or slapstick comedy into a situation. They often have traits that particularly appeal to children, such as rude behaviour, making smells and wearing underpants outside clothes!

Language, too, is an extremely important element of funny stories. As we enjoy the satisfaction of repetition in a rollicking rhyme or experience the delight of a new nonsense word or sound that really fits the situation, we cannot help chuckling to ourselves. Not only the sound of the words, but also the way they are portrayed on the page, can raise a laugh. We are all familiar with the way we feel compelled to alter the way we read when huge wiggling letters enclosed in a swirling speech bubble appear!

Funny stories vary according to the writing style of the authors. The three extracts in this section are good examples of different styles of humorous writing. Children are familiar with accessing humour through illustrations, but, by working with these three extracts, they can be encouraged to think about ways in which authors create humour through text.

Links to the Primary Framework

The Literacy Framework states that developing understanding of, and having opportunities to write, narrative texts is a fundamental aspect of children's literacy development. Narrative Units 1–4 within the Framework for Years 1 and 2 provide detailed guidance for teaching and learning about stories, focusing on familiar settings, a range of cultures, traditional tales and fairy tales and fantasy worlds. There are examples of funny stories within all of these, and children should have access to them. The activities in this book address objectives across the Literacy Framework with a particular focus on Strands 7–10 for Years 1 and 2.

Funny story features

Characters
- Amusing appearance.
- Outrageous behaviour.
- Behaving 'out of character'.
- Getting things wrong; making mistakes.
- Getting into muddles.
- Amusing traits, such as smells, silly walks.

Actions
- Slapstick humour.
- Surprises.
- Accidents.

Language
- Words chosen for comic effect.
- Rhyming text.
- Repetition.
- Nonsense words.
- Use of textual devices such as punctuation, shape and size of lettering.

Extract 1: Little Rabbit Foo Foo

This extract encourages children to realise that characters in funny stories do not always follow expectations.

- Open the extract from the CD-ROM. Read the story title, 'Little Rabbit Foo Foo', and discuss what this character might look like. Could it be a baby rabbit? Would Foo Foo have lots of woodland friends?

- Open 'What are they really like?' from the CD-ROM and type words showing what their expectations of Little Rabbit Foo Foo and the Good Fairy are before reading the extract. Save these and close.

- Read the extract together before underlining words that describe unexpected aspects of Foo Foo's character, such as 'riding', 'bopping', 'scooping up' and 'attitude'.

- Explore the image of 'The Good Fairy' and discuss expectations, asking appropriate questions, for example, *Will the Good Fairy grant three wishes? What might she say to Foo Foo?*

- Hand out copies of photocopiable page 14 'What are they really like?' and ask the children to complete it, following the steps they have already explored on screen.

- Come together to discuss how opinions of the characters in the two columns differ, focusing on unusual characteristics or actions.

Extract 2: The Day Jake Vacuumed

The second extract looks at wicked behaviour and presentational features that can emphasise these to create a funny story.

- Open the extract from the CD-ROM. Read it and discuss why Jake's behaviour is funny. Focus on a particular presentational aspect, for example, the use of capital letters and exclamation marks for 'BIG TROUBLE!' and 'POP!'. Highlight the chosen aspect on the text.

- Open 'Now you are in trouble!' from the CD-ROM. Ask the children to roll over the image of the vacuum cleaner and read the accompanying roll over text. Did Jake do as his mother asked? How did his mother react to his behaviour? Draw attention to speech marks.

- Do the same with the remaining image and discuss possible alternative actions and responses.

- Provide each child with a copy of photocopiable page 15 'Now you are in trouble!' to complete by writing sentences and illustrating Jake's possible reactions to his mother's requests, and her responses to these reactions. Decide together which ideas make the funniest story.

- Finally, choose one of the images together and read the accompanying request from Mum. Discuss a possible opening paragraph for a story based on this information. Tell this orally.

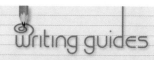

Extract 3: Up, Up and Away!

Exploring the third extract raises awareness of how an author's presentation of an amusing character can enhance a funny story.

What's on the CD-ROM

Up, Up and Away!
- Text extract to read, discuss and edit.

Little Rabbit Foo Foo, and The Day Jake Vacuumed
- Text extracts to read and discuss.

Mire Street Primary staff list
- Type descriptive words into boxes.

- Read the extract from the CD-ROM. What makes the teachers amusing? Draw attention to the teachers' characteristics and to the use of effective punctuation by annotating the text.

- Open 'Mire Street Primary staff list' from the CD-ROM. Explain that, when fully completed, it should give information about staff members. Read the name of the Reception class teacher and consider her possible appearance and character. Type words suggested by the children into the appropriate boxes.

- Decide together on suitable names for teachers of Class 3 and 4 and type their details into the appropriate boxes.

- Ask the children to work in groups, each with a computer or copy of photocopiable page 16 'Mire Street Primary staff list' to record their amusing ideas. Come together to decide who has created the funniest set of characters.

- Revisit all three extracts before handing out enlarged copies of photocopiable page 17 'Having a laugh'. Discuss what could be included in the boxes. Ask the children to complete this sheet to reinforce their awareness of what makes a funny story.

- Revisit the extract to discuss ways of editing it to enhance humour, for example, changing letter size and font, adding text and so on.

Poster: Funny stories

The poster summarises points discussed while completing the activities in this section.

What's on the CD-ROM

Funny stories
- Read and discuss information.
- Roll over sections to display additional text.

Little Rabbit Foo Foo, The Day Jake Vacuumed, and Up, Up and Away!
- Text extracts to read and discuss.

- Display the 'Funny stories' poster on the CD-ROM. Explain to the children that it will serve as a reminder of common features of many funny stories, and help them with their writing.

- Explore the artwork and the headings in zigzag boxes for each section to stimulate discussion about key features of the genre. Ask appropriate questions to encourage the children to make links between the pictures and the headings, for example, *What sort of mistake has this character made?* (Going out in the rain in a sun hat and flip-flops!) *What is wrong with baking a cake in a washing machine?*

- Roll your mouse over a section to display further text and read it together. Ask if the children can think of additional words or sounds that might be appropriate.

- Discuss each feature by referring to the three extracts. Point out those they have yet to explore in detail, such as slapstick and making mistakes. Ask them to suggest funny stories that contain such features.

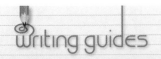

Extract 1: Little Rabbit Foo Foo

Little Rabbit Foo Foo riding through the forest, scooping up the field mice and bopping them on the head.

Down came the Good Fairy and said, "Little Rabbit Foo Foo, I don't like your attitude, scooping up the field mice and bopping them on the head. I'm going to give you three chances to change, and if you don't, I'm going to turn you into a goonie."

Little Rabbit Foo Foo riding through the forest, scooping up the wriggly worms and bopping them on the head.

Down came the Good Fairy and said…

Michael Rosen

Text © 1990, Michael Rosen; illustration © 2002, Arthur Robins.

Extract 2: The Day Jake Vacuumed

Jake was difficult. Jake was a problem. He never liked doing anything for anyone. So you can imagine how Jake felt when his mother asked him to do the vacuum cleaning. For a while Jake played with the machine, enjoying the loud noise it made.

Then a really wicked idea occurred to him. Very quietly he crept over to Timmy, the cat... Aiming the nozzle at Timmy, Jake switched on the cleaner and sucked up the poor cat! Jake was delighted.

He knew he would be in trouble, though.

"Well, if I'm going to be in trouble," he thought, "I might as well be in BIG TROUBLE!"

Six o'clock on the dot his father opened the front door. Out jumped Jake with the vacuum cleaner roaring on full power. It was difficult at first, but eventually... POP!

In went Jake's father.

"Hooray!" shouted Jake.

Jake was delighted.

Simon James

Text and illustration © 1989, Simon James.

Extract 3:
Up, Up and Away!

On the whole the teachers at Mire Street Primary were quite friendly. Well, all except two of them, that is – Mr Peabody and Miss Snapdragon.

Mr Peabody had a green complexion and a bushy moustache that attracted food like a magnet, while Miss Snapdragon was red from head to foot. Red hair, red clothes, red shoes…even red tissues for her constantly running red nose!

One morning the headteacher asked Mr Peabody and Miss Snapdragon to take their classes outside to use the large parachute. How those teachers hated going outside!

"**MARCH FORWARD!**" yelled Mr Peabody and Miss Snapdragon.

The children marched forward.

"**PLACES!**" yelled Mr Peabody and Miss Snapdragon.

The children took their places.

"**LIFT!**" shouted Mr Peabody and Miss Snapdragon.

Illustration © 2010, Mike Phillips/Beehive Illustration.

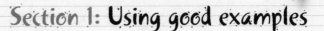
The children lifted the parachute.

Up and down, up and down, flip, flap, flip, flap.

"**MUSHROOM!**" shouted Mr Peabody and Miss Snapdragon.

The parachute billowed upwards to form a vast mushroom shape.

Ellie Pranks was first to run under to change places with Charlie Green standing opposite. But Ellie enjoyed playing tricks, just as her name suggests. She shuddered at the quivering moustache of Mr Peabody and smudged red lipstick of Miss Snapdragon. Enough was enough.

Time for a P-R-A-N-K!

She whispered to Charlie Green,

"*Let go at my signal. Pass it on.*"

Charlie grinned. Another prank from Ellie!

And so the message passed from one child to another beneath the billowing mushroom.

"*Ellie has a prank. Let go at her signal.*"

A gust of wind blew the mushroom while the children hung on tightly, watching Ellie Pranks.

"NOW!"

Ellie screamed and the children let go.

WHOOOOOOOOOSH!

SWISH! SWASH!

The mushroom left the ground with Mr Peabody and Miss Snapdragon hanging on.

"GET US DOWN!" wailed Mr Peabody and Miss Snapdragon.

Up, up and away, over the treetops they flew while the children cheered… and they carried on cheering until their friends came out to play.

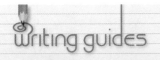

Photocopiable

What are they really like?

● What do you think of these characters? Write your ideas in the boxes.

	Before reading	**After reading**
Little Rabbit Foo Foo		
The Good Fairy		

Illustrations © 2002, Arthur Robins.

Now you are in trouble!

- Draw pictures in the boxes to show what is happening.
- Then follow the instructions in the top boxes.

1 What Mum might ask Jake to do.	**2** Write a sentence in each box about what Jake does instead.	**3** Write what Mum says to Jake in each box. Remember speech marks.
"Jake, will you do the vacuum cleaning?"		"You are in BIG TROUBLE!"
"Jake, will you feed Timmy, the cat?"		

Illustrations © 2010, Mike Phillips/Beehive Illustration.

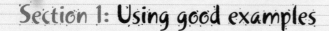

Section 1: Using good examples

Mire Street Primary staff list

- Invent names for other teachers and write them in their name boxes.
- Write words into the empty boxes for each teacher to describe their appearance and character.

Name of teacher	Position	Appearance	Character
Mrs Gringiggle	Reception teacher		
Miss Snapdragon	Class 1 teacher	runny red nose red hair red tissues	loves red strict no friends
Mr Peabody	Class 2 teacher	green complexion bushy moustache	huge voice strict no friends
	Class 3 teacher		
	Class 4 teacher		

Having a laugh

● Find and record examples from the three extracts of these funny moments.

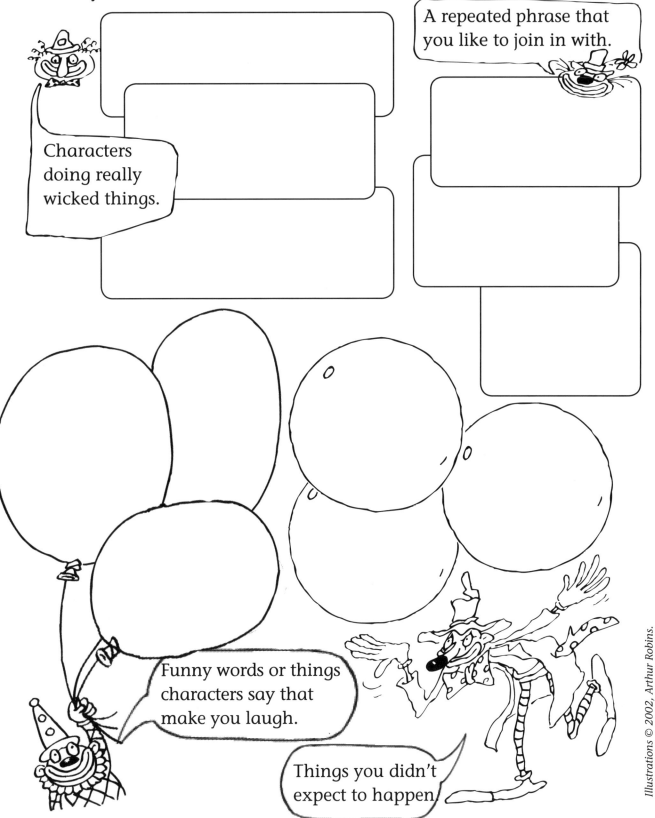

A repeated phrase that you like to join in with.

Characters doing really wicked things.

Funny words or things characters say that make you laugh.

Things you didn't expect to happen.

Illustrations © 2002, Arthur Robins.

Section 1: Using good examples

Funny stories

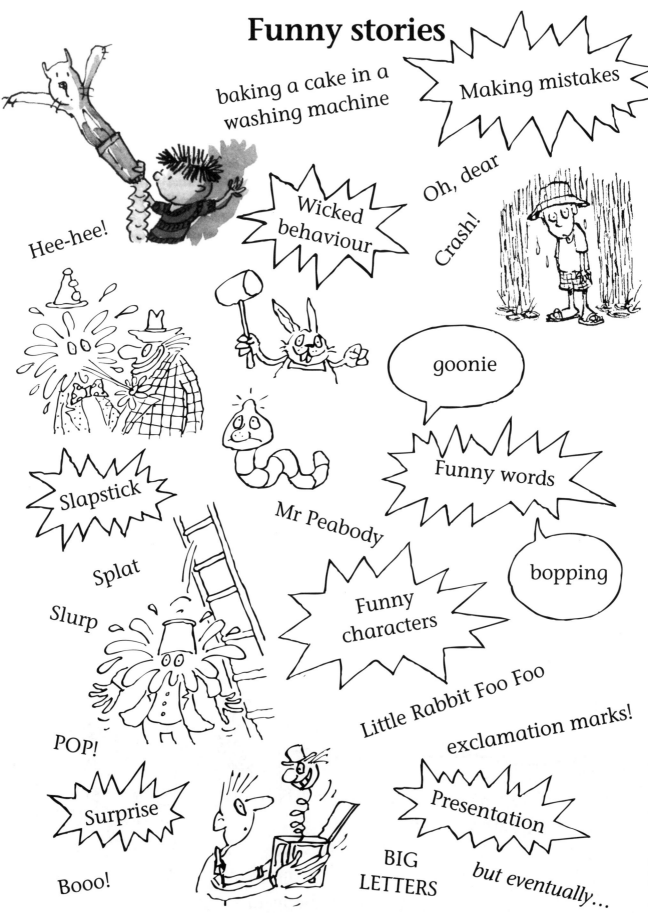

baking a cake in a washing machine

Making mistakes

Hee-hee!

Wicked behaviour

Oh, dear

Crash!

goonie

Slapstick

Mr Peabody

Funny words

Splat

Slurp

Funny characters

bopping

Little Rabbit Foo Foo

POP!

exclamation marks!

Surprise

Presentation

Booo!

BIG LETTERS

but eventually...

Top left illustration © 1989, Simon James; top right illustration © 2010, Mike Phillips/Beehive Illustration; other illustrations © 2002, Arthur Robins.

writing guides

Section 2

Developing writing

The activities in this section provide opportunities for children to explore the key elements of the funny stories genre in terms of character, setting and events. The weird and wonderful language of the funny stories genre is explored, with reference to rhyme, repetition, sound combinations and nonsense words, and children are encouraged to experiment with their own language ideas.

Character, setting and events

Children are given opportunities to explore a range of characters and to discuss and write about the ways in which their appearance, actions, language and behaviour contribute to the amusing elements of the story. They are also invited to take on the role of the characters in order to understand how they might react to different situations.

Children are encouraged to explore three familiar settings (a wood, kitchen and classroom), using photographs on the CD-ROM as stimulus, and consider how they could create an amusing situation by introducing a character to these settings. A photograph of a lunar landscape gives scope for further exploration of the role of fantasy in funny stories.

Everyday events can often become humorous when the unexpected happens. Children are invited to explore extracts on the CD-ROM and a selection of books to discover how humour has been injected into stories through accidents, surprises and unexpected behaviour. They are then asked to try these methods in their own stories.

How to use the activities

The teachers' notes give guidance on delivery, including how to use the photocopiable sheets and the materials on the CD-ROM. Children are encouraged to employ a range of strategies to introduce humour into their stories and a variety of simple writing templates are provided to support the development of their independent writing. Through discussion activities, retelling and role play, children have opportunities to review and modify their ideas before writing them down. The activities are flexible and can easily be adapted. All activities should be modelled to the whole class or smaller groups using the whiteboard before the children are asked to do independent work. The children's on-screen work and completed photocopiable sheets can be saved to form a resource bank of ideas for use when they start their story writing.

Activities breakdown

Character
- Out of the ordinary (page 20)
- Say that again (page 21)
- You are funny! (page 21)
- What made that noise? (page 22)
- Getting into mischief (page 23)

Setting
- Out of this world (page 24)
- Where did it happen? (page 24)

Events
- What a surprise! (page 20)
- Accidents will happen (page 22)
- Make it funny (page 23)

Activity 1: What a surprise!

Objective

To compose and write simple sentences independently to communicate meaning. (Year 1 Strand 11)

What's on the CD-ROM

The Day Jake Vacuumed
- Text extract to read and discuss.

Media resources
- Use images 'Wood', 'Classroom' and 'Kitchen' to explore settings and describe possible surprising events.

What to do

This activity encourages children to consider how the element of surprise contributes to humour, and asks them to devise their own 'surprises'.

- Explore a selection of story books and the CD-ROM extracts in which surprising events provide the humour, such as *Suddenly!* by Colin McNaughton (Collins Picture Lions) and *The Day Jake Vacuumed* (page 11).

- Explain to the children that they are going to think of their own surprises for stories. Remind them that these surprises should raise a laugh rather than be frightening.

- Explore the images from the CD-ROM for ideas for story settings. Consider surprising events that might happen to a character in each setting, for example, a rabbit hopping into a kitchen.

- Display photocopiable page 25 'What a surprise!'. Look at the images on the left and read the questions. Share ideas for surprises that may arise from each situation and think of words or phrases to accompany the right-hand image to reinforce the surprise, such as, 'Boo!'.

- Hand out copies of the photocopiable sheet and tell the children to complete the illustrations to show their imagined comic surprises, for example, the dustbin could explode in the rubbish collector's face. Add sentences or captions to explain the action.

Activity 2: Out of the ordinary

Objective

To make predictions showing an understanding of ideas, events and characters. (Year 1 Strand 7)

What's on the CD-ROM

Little Rabbit Foo Foo
- Text extract to read and discuss.

Out of the ordinary
- Drag and drop the words to appropriate images.

What to do

This activity will help children to identify links between humour and characters displaying uncharacteristic attributes.

- Read some books and the CD-ROM extracts where the central figure does not display the characteristics we would expect but is considered 'out of the ordinary', for example, *Princess Smartypants* by Babette Cole (Picture Puffin) and *Little Rabbit Foo Foo* (page 10). What might our usual expectations of the characters be? What happens that goes against these expectations?

- Open 'Out of the ordinary' from the CD-ROM and look at the characters. Read the words and identify which characters they are associated with. Drag and drop the words into the correct image boxes.

- Think of 'out of the ordinary' characteristics for the characters on the right, for example, a 'furry' baby or a 'shy' witch.

- Provide copies of the photocopiable sheet and ask the children to draw pictures of invented characters in the appropriate boxes. Then ask them to write words to describe what is out of the ordinary about the character. Invite the children to show and describe their characters.

Activity 3: Say that again

Objective

To explore the effect of patterns of language and repeated words and phrases. (Year 1 Strand 7)

What's on the CD-ROM

Funny titles
- Drag and drop words to complete funny rhyming titles on book covers.

What to do

This activity stimulates children's awareness of how rhyme, rhythm and repetition can introduce humour into a story.

- Explore a selection of rhyming stories with amusing titles chosen for comic effect, for example, *Room on the Broom* by Julia Donaldson (Macmillan Children's Books), *All Afloat on Noah's Boat* by Tony Mitton (Orchard Books). Explore the titles and illustrations and identify rhyming words, repeated phrases and nonsense words that add to the humour. Ask the children to say which book they like best and why.

- Open 'Funny titles' from the CD-ROM. Read the instructions with the class and invite the children to read the partially completed titles. Can they think of suitable rhyming words to complete them? Read the words at the bottom of the screen and drag and drop appropriate rhyming words to complete the titles.

- Provide each child with a copy of photocopiable page 27 'Funny titles'. Invite them to finish the partially completed book titles, write their own funny titles on the two empty covers and illustrate all the covers.

Activity 4: You are funny!

Objective

To explore familiar themes and characters through improvisation and role play. (Year 1 Strand 4)

What's on the CD-ROM

Little Rabbit Foo Foo, and The Day Jake Vacuumed
- Text extracts to read and discuss.

You are funny!
- Drag and drop the names of characters to show what things make them funny.

What to do

This activity encourages children to explore the appearance, behaviour and language of funny characters through group discussion and role play.

- Open 'Little Rabbit Foo Foo' from the CD-ROM. Read it together and discuss what it tells us about the character.

- Open 'You are funny!' from the CD-ROM and read the instructions with the class. Invite the children to drag the characters' names under the headings to describe what they think makes the characters funny.

- Then read the extract 'The Day Jake Vacuumed', before completing the section about Jake.

- Provide a selection of dressing-up clothes and accessories and invite the children to work in small groups to invent a funny character. Supply each group with individual copies of photocopiable page 28 'You are funny!'. Ask them to finish the top section of the sheet independently and then collaborate to complete the section about their invented character.

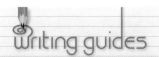

Activity 5: Accidents will happen!

Objective

To group written sentences together in chunks of meaning or subject. (Year 1 Strand 10)

What to do

This activity explores the way in which minor accidents can be interpreted as funny incidents.

● Slapstick is a feature of much of children's humour. Explain to the children that slapstick involves characters falling, slipping and crashing or bumping into things in an exaggerated and humorous way, without actually being hurt. (Emphasise that the incidents may not be so funny if they actually happened as someone could be injured.)

● Display photocopiable page 29 'Accidents will happen!' and read the sentence under the first example. Invite the children to suggest an appropriate sentence to describe the picture depicting the boy slipping on the banana skin. Draw attention to the way the two sentences follow one another to tell a story. Discuss possible events that might follow the next two incidents.

● Encourage the children to use the empty boxes at the bottom to write their own 'accident' sentence and an amusing consequence.

● Provide each child with a copy of the photocopiable sheet to complete by following the instructions and recalling the whole-class activity.

Activity 6: What made that noise?

Objective

To select from different presentational features to suit particular writing purposes on paper and on screen. (Year 2 Strand 9)

What's on the CD-ROM

Little Rabbit Foo Foo, and Up, Up and Away!
● Text extracts to read and discuss.

What made that noise?
● Drag and drop sound words to match pictures.

What to do

This activity introduces different ways of representing sounds within stories.

● Explain that the children are going to think of ways of representing sounds in their funny stories.

● Open the 'Little Rabbit Foo Foo' extract from the CD-ROM and ask the children which word represents the noise of Little Rabbit Foo Foo hitting mice. Think of alternative words for 'bopped', for example, 'biffed', 'banged', 'clattered'. Do the same with the extract, 'Up, Up and Away!', focusing on the sounds of the parachute – 'WHOOOOOOOOOSH!' 'SWISH!' and 'SWASH!'.

● Open 'What made that noise?' from the CD-ROM. Look at the pictures together and read the words. Decide which words most effectively describe the sounds made in the pictures. Then drag and drop these words to the correct pictures.

● Provide individual copies of photocopiable page 30 'What made that noise?' and ask the children to add one or more cartoon-style words to each picture to represent the sounds being made.

Activity 7: Make it funny

Objective

To adopt appropriate roles in small or large groups and consider alternative courses of action.
(Year 2 Strand 4)

What's on the CD-ROM

The Day Jake Vacuumed, and Up, Up and Away!
● Extracts to discuss and compare.

What to do

This activity encourages children to create amusing situations by moving away from the obvious and adopting alternative courses.

● Select one of the extracts and invite the children to consider how an alternative course of action caused amusement. For example, when Jake sucked up family members with the vacuum cleaner instead of cleaning, or when the school parachute transported two unpopular teachers far away.

● Display photocopiable page 31 'Make it funny' and look at the picture in the left-hand column showing the ordinary action of bathing a baby. Discuss what has happened in the right-hand picture to turn this action into a funny situation.

● Read the captions under the empty boxes and ask the children to work in small groups to discuss how these actions might become funny situations. Suggest that they choose one of the actions to dramatise, first as an ordinary event and then as an amusing situation.

● Come back together and watch the groups' dramatisations and discuss whether they make others laugh.

● Provide each child with a copy of the photocopiable sheet to complete. Read the instructions together to ensure that they know what to do.

Activity 8: Getting into mischief

Objective

To tell real or imagined stories using the conventions of familiar story language.
(Year 2 Strand 1)

What's on the CD-ROM

Getting into mischief
● Click on two cards to select a character and an object.

What to do

This activity encourages children to make up funny stories about what mischievous characters can do with everyday props.

● Remind the children that funny characters often get up to mischief. Recap the antics of Jake and Little Rabbit Foo Foo and the role of props or objects in their actions. Recall how an ordinary vacuum cleaner in Jake's hands resulted in hilarious events.

● Open 'Getting into mischief' from the CD-ROM. Explain that the cards have characters and objects on them. Invite a child to click on one of each type of card to reveal two images. Ask the children to identify the character and prop and suggest an amusing incident.

● Choose another child to reveal a different character and object. Together, think of something mischievous for this character to do with the object, for example, an elephant tipping a bucket of water over a zookeeper. Repeat until all the children have had a turn.

● Provide groups with photocopiable page 32 'Getting into mischief', to share. Ask them to cut out the pictures and put them into two piles of characters and objects. They should select one card from each pile and use them to write their own funny stories.

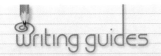
writing guides

Activity 9: Out of this world

What to do

This activity encourages children to invent amusing stories set in fantasy worlds.

- Explore stories relating to aliens, such as, *Here Come the Aliens!* by Colin McNaughton (Walker Books). Discuss how the illustrations and text make these stories amusing rather than frightening. Focus on humorous aspects of aliens, such as what they eat and their nonsense, rhythmic speech.

- Explore the 'Lunar landscape' image from the CD-ROM. Decide what type of amusing creatures might live there.

- Display photocopiable page 33 'Out of this world' and discuss together who might live on this planet. Consider things such as appearance and how the creatures might behave.

- Listen to the 'Swanee whistle' audio and consider whether this is the sort of sound an alien might make. Try to imitate it and suggest other noises suitable for such creatures.

- Provide each child with a copy of photocopiable page 33 'Out of this world'. Invite them to add colour to enhance the landscape, draw a family of amusing lunar creatures on separate paper, cut them out and stick them to the page. Add speech bubbles in the same way.

Activity 10: Where did it happen?

What to do

This activity encourages children to work together to create an amusing story, given a character and setting.

- Select the four images in turn from 'Media resources' and consider amusing situations that could be set in each one.

- Display photocopiable page 34 'Where did it happen?' and ask the children to name the possible settings and characters. Explain that they are going to work in groups to act out an amusing play based on a given character and setting.

- Provide each group with the photocopiable sheet. Ask them to cut out the pictures and divide them into two piles, 'characters' and 'settings'. Then spread out each pile, turn them upside down and shuffle them around. The children can then pick one card from each pile and start to invent their play based on the chosen character and setting.

- Interact with the groups as they work, suggesting that they delegate some tasks, such as scribing, finding costumes and making props. Supply the items needed as far as possible.

- Watch the performances and constructively criticise productions.

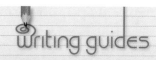

What a surprise!

● Complete the pictures in the second column to show how these characters were surprised.

● Write a sentence about what happened in the box below each picture.

| What happened when the rubbish collector took off the dustbin lid? | |

| What happened when Dad took the pie out of the oven? | |

| What happened when the frog woke from a nap under the teacher's desk? | |

Out of the ordinary

● Draw pictures in the boxes to show funny versions of these characters.

Ordinary characters	Out of the ordinary characters
A witch	A funny witch
A baby	A funny baby
A princess	A funny princess
A frog	A funny frog

Funny titles

- Choose words from the bottom of the page to create rhyming titles for the two incomplete book covers.
- Make up your own funny titles for the empty book covers.
- Complete all the book covers by adding funny illustrations.

THANK FRANK FOR HIS SILLY ....

Ellie Kelly makes worm ....

| soup | trick | jelly | joke | stew | prank |

You are funny!

● What makes these characters funny? Put a tick in the box under the heading that you think describes the funniest thing about each character.

Name	Behaviour	Appearance	Funny words
Little Rabbit Foo Foo	☐	☐	☐
The Good Fairy	☐	☐	☐
Jake	☐	☐	☐

● Draw a picture of a funny character you have invented in the space below and then fill in the boxes to describe your character.

Name	Behaviour	Appearance	Funny words

Writing guides

Accidents will happen!

● Add pictures and captions to show what happened next.

Michael ran along the path, straight towards the banana skin.

Rabbit hopped along the road, but didn't see the open manhole.

Parvesh walked through the woods, looking over his shoulder.

What made that noise?

● Choose a word from the bottom of the page – or one of your own – to show the sound being made in each picture.

writing guides

Make it funny

● Look at the actions described on the left and draw pictures about them. Think of other ways of carrying out these actions to create a funny situation.

● Write a sentence and draw a picture about each idea in the right-hand column. The first one has been done for you.

The action	The other action
 Bathing a baby.	 Spilling a whole bottle of bubble bath into the bath.
Getting dressed.	
Carrying a balloon.	

Getting into mischief

● Colour the pictures on this page and cut them out to create a set of cards.

Illustrations © 2002, Arthur Robins.

Section 2: Developing writing

Out of this world

- Colour in this page to make it even more unusual.
- Think of funny alien creatures that might live in this fantasy landscape. Draw them on white paper, cut them out and stick them on the page.
- Add speech bubbles in the same way to show their nonsense words and sounds.

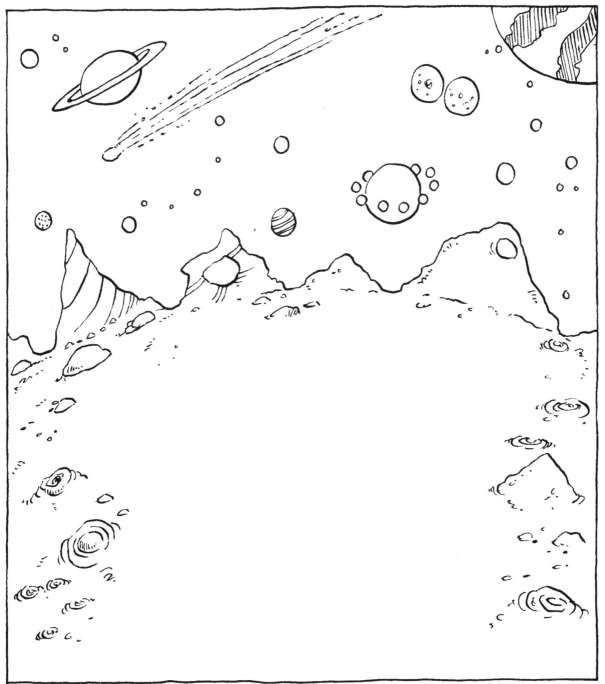

Illustration © 2010, Mike Phillips/Beehive Illustration.

SCHOLASTIC
www.scholastic.co.uk

Where did it happen?

● Cut out the cards. Put them in two piles, a pile of characters and a pile of settings for stories.

Character	Setting

Illustrations © 2010, Mike Phillips/Beehive Illustration.

writing guides

Writing

Creative process

Having discussed and shared examples of funny stories, and worked through the activities in Section 2, the children should now be aware of key features for this genre and be ready to start writing their own funny stories.

The three writing projects in this section provide opportunities for the children to plan and write funny stories, and the activities within them will actively encourage the development of their story-writing skills.

It is important to be flexible when allocating time for each project as the children will need to progress from their initial ideas to the finished stories. Several extended writing sessions may be needed to allow for planning, drafting, redrafting and 'publishing' of stories. How many will depend on the children. Some will happily revisit their developing work over several sessions, while others will find revisiting unfinished work in order to move forward much more difficult. These children will need more time and support so that they can develop the necessary skills to restart or redraft their work with growing confidence.

Planning the sessions

The three writing projects in this section all progress along a similar format, providing the children with the following opportunities:

- Oral sessions to discuss and rehearse ideas in pairs, small groups and the whole class.

- Shared sessions to use planning frames to convert shared ideas for funny scenarios into written text using the 'My funny story' writing templates on the CD-ROM.

- Independent sessions to work alone, repeating the work done in the shared session, planning and writing individual funny stories. These stories can be presented on screen using 'My funny story' writing templates, or on paper as extended writing.

Providing support

Ensure that appropriate support is given to individuals throughout the whole writing process. Refer the children back to the poster, 'Funny stories' (on the CD-ROM or photocopiable page 18), for further ideas when planning and drafting their stories. Recall particular activities from previous sessions to support specific aspects, for example, using appropriate presentation techniques ('What made that noise?' page 22). As well as providing different contexts for writing, motivate children by introducing a range of formats for presenting work, for example, individual computers, books, paper of different colours and sizes, decorative borders and so on.

Writing tips

When writing a funny story consider introducing:
- 'out of the ordinary' characters
- wicked or mischievous behaviour
- inexperienced characters
- slapstick comedy
- mistakes
- surprises
- funny words
- nonsense sounds
- repetition
- punctuation, such as exclamation marks
- presentation techniques, such as speech bubbles and varying lettering size and font.

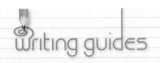

Project 1: How funny you are!

What to do

This activity teaches children how to write a funny story using the planning and writing templates on the CD-ROM. Initial focus is on the main character.

- Display photocopiable page 39 'How funny you are!'. Look at the book covers and read the descriptions underneath the covers and discuss suitable main characters and story titles together. Remind the children that the book will be a funny one.

- Provide each child with photocopiable page 39 'How funny you are!' to complete on their own. Explain that they will be writing a story about one of the funny characters they have invented afterwards.

- Explore the four images of settings on the CD-ROM and discuss how their invented characters could fit into them.

- Open the 'Story planner' from the CD-ROM. Complete the four screens of the planner together. Starting with the main character, invite the children to choose one from their completed sheets. Discuss and type in a suitable setting, story opening, event(s) and ending. Finally, agree on a title.

- Open 'My funny story' from the CD-ROM and choose one of the writing templates. Explain that this will be the first page of the story. Show the children how to drag and drop an image from the 'Image bank' on to the page and demonstrate how to resize it (it is possible to upload extra images into the bank if children wish to). Type a short opening for a funny story into the box below, using the children's ideas. Remind them that a story opening should introduce the main character(s) and setting.

- Open the next page (template) by clicking on 'Add page'. Continue the story in the same way by selecting page layouts, choosing images, orally drafting and finally writing text into text boxes.

- Explore the different tools available to enhance the humorous presentation of the story, for example, adding speech bubbles.

- Explain how to use the 'Cover' template on the CD-ROM to design a suitable cover.

- Read the finished story with the children and discuss content and presentation. How funny is it? Could it be even funnier? Make changes until the children are satisfied with the story they have created.

- Ask each child to choose a book cover from the previously completed photocopiable sheet, and provide them with a copy of photocopiable page 38 'Story planner'. Invite them to plan and write a funny story based on their chosen title and main character.

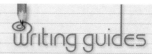

Project 2: Fantasy worlds

What to do

This activity reinforces story-writing skills by asking children to compose funny stories set in fantasy worlds.

- Read some funny stories set in fantasy worlds, for example, *Aliens Love Underpants* by Claire Freedman (Simon & Schuster). Look at the 'Lunar landscape' image on the CD-ROM and discuss how humour could be injected into this setting by introducing amusing characters.

- Display photocopiable page 40 'Where do you live?' and talk about the character and setting in the first box. Consider possible settings for the other boxes and characters who might live there. Let the children complete the photocopiable sheet following the shared discussions.

- Open the 'Story planner' from the CD-ROM. Create a shared story plan about a character and setting using the photocopiable sheet.

- Open 'My funny story' from the CD-ROM (see Project 1 for instructions for use). Write the planned story together.

- Using photocopiable page 38 'Story planner', let the children plan and write their own story about a funny character living in a fantasy world, referring to their ideas on photocopiable page 40.

Project 3: Fun at school

What to do

This activity encourages children to focus on humorous language as they write a school-based story.

- Open 'Make me laugh!' from the CD-ROM. Read the headings and recall how words can make stories funnier. Invite the children to choose words to drag and drop into the appropriate boxes.

- Provide copies of photocopiable page 41 'Make me laugh' to complete. The children can add new words if they wish to.

- Read the extract 'Up, Up and Away!' and explore the image of a classroom on the CD-ROM. Suggest writing a similar school-based story. Open 'School plan 1' from the CD-ROM and ask the children to plan a story that takes place in different parts of this school. Think about funny events that could take place. Roll over the different areas on the plan to reveal text to stimulate the children's ideas for discussion.

- Invite children to compose a school-based funny story as a piece of extended writing, or use the writing templates on the CD-ROM (see Project 1) and photocopiable pages 42 'School plan 1' and 43 'School plan 2'.

Story planner

- Plan and write your own funny story.

Main character: _____

Other characters: _____

Setting: _____
_____

Story opening: _____
_____

Events:

1 _____

2 _____

3 _____

Story ending: _____
_____

Title: _____
_____

How funny you are!

- Read the description for each book.
- Invent a title for each book cover. Then draw the main character on the back cover.

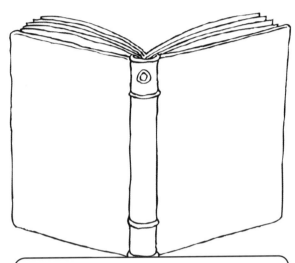

This funny character is full of mischief and fond of playing wicked tricks using a prop.

This funny character has lots of surprises in store!

This funny character makes mistakes and gets into muddles.

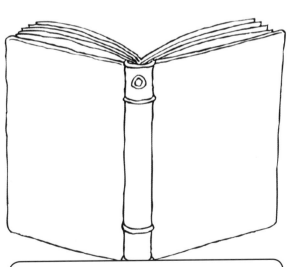

This funny character looks very unusual.

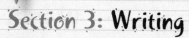
Where do you live?

- Look at the funny character in her story setting in the first box.
- In the other boxes draw your own pictures of the characters in their setting.
- Write the characters' names in the boxes below each picture.

I live in a cave at the bottom of the ocean.

My name is Flora Fin

I live on a far distant planet.

My name is _____

I live in the time of dinosaurs.

My name is _____

I live in a world of dragons.

My name is _____

Illustration © 2010, Mike Phillips/Beehive Illustration.

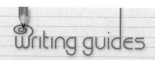

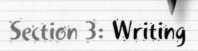
SCHOLASTIC Photocopiable
www.scholastic.co.uk

Make me laugh

- Read the headings for each box.
- Do you think the words in each box match the headings?
- Read the words at the bottom of the page and write them in the boxes you think are the most suitable.

Words for sounds	Nonsense words	Rhyming words
RROARRRRR! buzzzzz	ninglydop frozzly	tickle pickle
Words for surprises	**Silly names**	**Silly movements**
yoooo! surprise!	jelly belly goonie	kerplunk wiggly

zzzzzzzz   twotoe   roly   hobble   strizzle   BOO!   scrunch

ombix   flip-flap   honkalot   suddenly!   poly

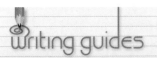

School plan 1

- Use this page with 'School plan 2' to make notes about your funny school story.
- Look at the school plan and choose three places where funny events might take place.
- Number the places 1, 2 and 3 and draw a line to join them.

Head teacher's office

Reception

Hall

Kitchen

Year 1

Year 2

Year 3

Year 4

Playground

Illustration © 2010, Mike Phillips/Beehive Illustration.

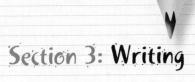
School plan 2

● Use this page with 'School plan 1' to make notes about your funny school story.

● Answer the questions below.

Where in the school does your story start?

_____

What happens in the place you have marked number 1?

_____

_____

What happens in the place you have marked number 2?

_____

_____

What happens in the place you have marked number 3?

_____

_____

Where does the story finish?

_____

Think of funny ways that your character might move
from one part of the school to the next as the story unfolds.
Write your ideas here.

_____

_____

_____

What time of day does the story take place?

_____

Review

Ongoing assessment of children's writing skills is vital. It enables you to monitor individual progress towards specific learning targets and to plan the next steps for learning at the children's own level. Equally relevant is the reviewing of overall progress at the end of a unit of work in order to identify areas of teaching and learning that need to be reinforced or modified.

Self review

The children should be encouraged to engage in a process of self review. Photocopiable page 45 'Self review' has been designed to be used by children independently in order to decide how successful they have been in introducing features of the funny story genre into their own writing. Demonstrate how to use the page initially to review a story that you have created together.

Peer review

Photocopiable page 46 'Peer review' involves working with writing partners of a similar ability to motivate children to review and redraft their written work. Explain to the children that they should answer the questions on the photocopiable sheet. This will enable their partners to gain feedback on how well their stories engage the reader and whether or not the humour is universally appreciated. Discuss the children's roles as writing partners beforehand to ensure that their comments are constructive and supportive.

Teacher review

The assessment of the children's stories should focus on their use of key features of funny stories explored in the previous sections. However, the generic skills of story writing can also form part of the assessment. For example, in reviewing the children's work during the drafting process, you may need to remind them to ensure that their story structure remains clear, with a beginning, one or more events and an ending. This can sometimes be forgotten as the children get carried away with the humour, which in turn can become quite surreal or ridiculous rather than universally amusing.

Photocopiable page 47 'Teacher review' has been designed to enable you to record evidence of children's progress and attainment at the end of a unit of work on funny stories. It is linked to the eight writing Assessment Focuses.

As you consider children's work in relation to each Assessment Focus, it is essential to look at different types of evidence, for example, the language children use, their ability to take on dramatic roles or their contributions to shared discussions. A child that easily slips into a fantasy role or confidently expresses ideas orally, may not be so sure when it comes to writing ideas down, whereas another child will be quite the opposite.

Self review

● Read your story and complete the sections below.

My funny story is called: _____

Beginning

My story has a clear beginning that introduces the main character and setting.

Yes ☐   No ☐

Funny characters

The main character is called: _____

This character is funny because: _____

I have called some of the other characters: _____

_____

Funny events

The funniest thing that happens in my story is:

_____

Funny language

I have used these words to make my story funny:

_____

Presentation

I have used letters of different sizes and shapes for effect. ☐

I have used punctuation for effect, such as exclamation marks. ☐

I have used special effects, such as speech bubbles or shout boxes. ☐

Peer review

● Answer these questions to review your partner's funny story.

Story title: _____.

Written by: _____.

Beginning
The start of the story introduces the main
character and setting.   Yes ☐ No ☐

Characters
The main character makes me laugh.   Yes ☐ No ☐

Events
Some of the things that happen make
me laugh.   Yes ☐ No ☐

Language
Some of the words are funny.   Yes ☐ No ☐

Presentation
The story has some special effects that
make it even funnier.   Yes ☐ No ☐

What did you like best about the story?

_____

Describe one thing that you think would improve the story.

_____

_____

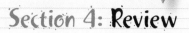

Teacher review

	AF5 Vary sentences for clarity, purpose and effect.	AF6 Write with technical accuracy of syntax and punctuation in phrases, clauses and sentences.	AF3 Organise and present whole texts effectively, sequencing and structuring information, ideas and events.	AF4 Construct paragraphs and use cohesion within and between paragraphs.	AF1 Write imaginative, interesting and thoughtful texts.	AF2 Produce texts that are appropriate to task, reader and purpose.	AF7 Select appropriate and effective vocabulary.	AF8 Use correct spelling.
LEVEL 1	Using simple phrases and clauses for humorous effect. Beginning to create sentences by joining clauses using connectives.	Clauses are mostly grammatically accurate. Some correct use of full stops and capital letters.	Events sequenced in appropriate order. Story openings and endings generally appropriate to genre, for example, 'Poof, he was gone!'.	Some events and ideas linked by repetition of words/ phrases to enhance humour.	Information about characters and events portrayed by vocabulary, for example, Snifflesnonk. Some simple descriptive vocabulary used to enhance humorous element.	Some key features of funny stories used in own stories.	Use of appropriate simple vocabulary with some effective word and sound choices, for example, 'Yarool' and 'Sssssss!'. Some humour injected through repetition of words and sounds.	Some high frequency words spelled correctly. Some attempts to spell nonsense words and sounds phonetically.
LEVEL 2	Some variation in sentence opening for humorous effect, such as, 'Boool' and 'Suddenly'. Simple sentence structure with some use of 'and' and 'but' as connectives. Generally consistent use of past and present tenses.	Sentence demarcation using full stops and capital letters is generally accurate. Some accurate use of exclamation marks and question marks to assist humour.	Some simple sequencing of events and ideas, for example, gradually developing actions to a humorous climax. Opening or closing sometimes signalled by varied presentation techniques, for example, bold capitals.	Planning frames used to connect ideas. Some events and ideas linked by repetition to enhance humour.	Content and ideas is usually relevant, with repetition used to appropriate effect. Features from favourite funny stories explored together sometimes apparent in own stories.	Some attempts at an appropriate style for genre. General awareness of key features shown.	Some use of speech bubbles to communicate a character's humorous vocabulary. Some adventurous word choices and introduction of nonsense words for effect.	Most high frequency words spelled correctly. Spelling of unknown and made-up words demonstrating increasing knowledge of word structure and spelling patterns.

Also available in this series:

ISBN 978-1407-11253-4

ISBN 978-1407-11265-7

ISBN 978-1407-11267-1

ISBN 978-1407-11256-5

ISBN 978-1407-11270-1

ISBN 978-1407-11248-0

ISBN 978-1407-11254-1

ISBN 978-1407-11266-4

ISBN 978-1407-11258-9

ISBN 978-1407-11268-8

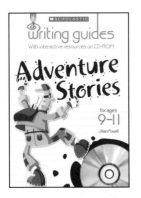

ISBN 978-1407-11251-0

ISBN 978-1407-11257-2

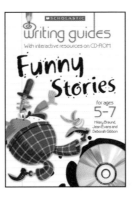

ISBN 978-1407-11255-8

ISBN 978-1407-11269-5

ISBN 978-1407-11250-3

ISBN 978-1407-11247-3

ISBN 978-1407-11252-7

ISBN 978-1407-11264-0

To find out more, call: **0845 603 9091** or visit our website: **www.scholastic.co.uk**